Days Forgone

A Collection of Life-Touching Poems

Arupratan Chakrabarti

BookLeaf Publishing

India | USA | UK

Made with ❤ on the BookLeaf Publishing Platform
www.bookleafpub.in
www.bookleafpub.com

Dedication

This collection of poems is dedicated to
Anindyasundar, Abhirup, Sumita, and all my beloved
readers who like to read
poems.

Preface

"Days Forgone—*A Collection of Life-Touching Poems* " is a blend of unique ideas, deep thoughts, lovely nature, and unforgettable moments of life. Philosophy of living and feelings of love elevate our minds to the next level of existence.

Author Arupratan Chakrabarti was greatly influenced by the guidance of his father, Anil Kumar Chakrabarti. Arupratan chakrabarti used to read English poems from childhood and likes to write lyrical poems in Bengali and English. His almost 28 years of teaching experience under the Higher Education Department of Tripura, India, make him a keen observer of heart-touching life events. Readers can enjoy the journey with the poems reflecting the true emotions of life.

Acknowledgements

I love poems, I write poems, and I am always with poems but publishing a book is an opportunity to share my thoughts with all of my readers. My heartfelt gratitude to Booklief Publishing. Their unique support and readers' appreciation are deeply valued. Regards to my father Anil Kumar Chakravarty for his support and special thanks to all of my readers, who are my inspiration.

The first note out of the silence

Music comes out of the silence
Every note you write
On your absent mind
Creates a garland of sound behind.

Music loves the heart,
Emotion burst out of the concert
Have the power to submerge
Feelings of life to convert.

The blue sky is full of sound
Expressed or unexpressed so profound
Can fill the atmos of the universe.
The nature is musical with lyrical verse.

The rhythm of heart aligns with the
Pulse of universe
Nature never disturbs us
But we can create
Chaotic unnatural sound out of our brain.
We tend to be musical
To fly free with our mind

On the way of life, as nature trains.

Forgetfulness

To forget, can you forgive?
Always remembering is a pain to the soul
Love knows no bindings,
Freedom is the reflection of truthfulness,
Administrator forgets emotion,
True businessman forgets profit or loss,
Humanity represents expanding acceptance.
The practice of cruelty and intolerance
cannot forgive you, as you cannot forget that.
You are blessed by forgetfulness,
When your mind is full of simplicity.
Forget all ugly matters and in the vacuum of
forgetfulness
The mind will be ready to remember
The Holi aspect of existence.
Submerged in the ocean of peace
A feeling of fulfilment prevails,
And you have to avoid all the limitations
Which creates friction in the momentum of life.

Depth of the dark

Oh! It is midnight
The time dreams
For the dawn --
First emerging light
From the east horizon.

If you are still awake,
Keeping head
On the lap of darkness,
Listen, silently, to the story
Of the days forgone.

Becoming

Silent night echoes
From the darkness
---Free you are free
Sunlight reveals the truth
---nature is Almighty.
Self-arrested we are
Eager to become infinity.

Lovely Light

Lovely winter morning
Reminds me of you, my dear.
Loving drops of dew
On the soft green grass,
Lovely lights from the Sun
Hugs to the glowing leaves.
Beneath the tree, I feel winds
Blowing gently and whispering
Some notes of love.
Not near the ocean,
Not in the mountains,
Dwelling on a plain land
Seating on the green grass
Near the paddy field
Thinking about you, my love
Lovely hue of green
Hug nature with affectionate bliss.

Love Unlimited

O my dear, far or near
Anywhere you stay.
I can feel you anytime
That is the power of love
So subtle, so quick, so intense
That you can hear
The call of my heart.

Through the dunes of the desert
Let us play hide and seek,
Over the green blue valley
The mountain wall echoes my voice,
I call you; you look back
While going to collect water
from the downstream.

In the dense forest
Among the sound of so many creatures
My voice you can hear so clear
If the relation follows the rule
And the victim is convicted
We will arrest ourselves forever.

Maybe the winter has come

Flakes of snow decorating
The background of our selfie
Our whisper will be louder
Than the falling sound
Of the leaf during the spring.

If it is a shiny summer
Let us find each other
On the seashore, waves of
Blue Ocean will resemble
Unfurled wishes ever exposed.

Relation

Freedom feels infinity,
Purity gives us peace,
Happiness comes out of acceptance,
Stress ---singing can seize.

Busy

Radish orange was the
Colour of the western sky
Announcing the closing of the day
I was busy with chatting
Yellowish white was the
Colour of the eastern sky
Announcing the opening of the day
I was lazy enough with my eyes closed
You called me to go with you
In the middle of the day
But alas! I am unable to go
As duties and works are yet to be done.

Our Home

At last, we go back to our home.
Our sweet home,
Designed with our loving things
There is a room in the home
Personal, reflecting all that I like,
One pen and a diary
To prepare plans that I wish
I take a rest on the lap of the night
With a full stop to the daydreams
With sense awake
I sit calm and quiet
my resting mind and relaxed body
feels the smile of silence.
Now, the mind lands on a magic land.
Which rejuvenates towards a new dawn.
Morning light comes through the window
Of my home, my sweet home.

On the lap of nature

I am floating on the pond water
You can come with me
Free to go near the water lily
White purple pink and so on
Reflecting on the water's surface
Diluted by the waves created by my ores
Again, it is clear and still
When I am sitting silently
On the boat.
The musical sound of the birds
Amplified by the flowing wind
Making happy all the green trees
On the bank,
I am floating with thoughts haunting-
Who is there, just behind the
Beautiful nature, we are living on behalf of.

Holi Love

Love never fails
Love is omnipotent
Failure comes with bloody fleshy feelings
But let's mind it
Mind can keep us high
Above the struggle of existence
Quarrel and disagreement cannot hamper
The essence of pure love.
Let's come nearer to the soul
And feel the peace of mind.
The magic of love sounds so sweet
Out of purity and freedom
You can have the permit
To love to the extent of infinity
That makes you the happiest in the world.

Where to rest

When the sky is the ocean
Ether creates waves of infinite
All the stars are floating ship
The voyager is from the east to the west bank.
"Full of sound and fury"
Life passes by and ends to exist.
O dear, where to sit
Let us become a dual star
In the family of starship.
And share the words that come out of
Our loving mind.
Where to rest in the moving world
Amongst the thousands of starships.
Let us live with unparalleled credentials,
Enjoying the maturity we reap.

Mom's Daughter

From far behind my senses
I bless you, my daughter,
The core of my heart is full of you.
God has given you wings to fly
The wind of my wish will blow
Anywhere you want to flow.
People come people go
Nobody may stand by you,
But my little baby, Glide alone
To show your courage above all
Reflected light of my thoughts
Is a lighthouse to guide you, baby doll,
Through the dark sea of
Duties and works of your life
I love your spirit of performance,
Your endeavour towards the new dawn
Along with a conceptual sense
Your great attitude toward the world
Be the ever-lovely herald
Your face is reflecting me
My child, love you, love me, love Thee.

When Life is a Drama

Full of fun and fury, the life you lead, O professor,
Your emotion became drama,
Your administration became the story,
Being a central character of your life,
Tragedy and catharsis are the swing of your hand.
You enjoyed days with smoke, life with feelings.
Expression of your oriented love was omnipotent.

People were observed thoroughly through your eyes,
Innovative thoughts were the result of research.
Your brain was truthful to the north like a compass.
Every footstep relates to the acting in your life drama.
O professor, your pure feelings, of true knowledge,
are always searching for a favourable environment.
The core of your heart is the abode of regret, silence,
Submission, sorrow, and enjoyment.

Co-characters of your life drama were better half,
Family members, friends, colleagues, people around you,
even street mads. But loneliness overwhelmed you.
Blessed with the shower of respect, alone by your heart,
You know the future; you can judge the situation better.
You can manage every standard of life.
But O professor, you do not know how cruel the reality

is!
And you do not know the director of your direction.
Till, after the last breath, you will be submerged in the
Poetic love-sense of John Keats,
Dramatic irony of Bernard Shaw,
Once and again, you will remember the story of your life
Passed with your beloved family members.

Mid Night O'clock

Silence of night
Covers the nature
With a dark black cloth,
Only owl can see.

Darkness prevails
Like a magic
In the depth of sleep.
All hypnotised to rejuvenate
And awake up with a new show
Of tomorrow.

It is midnight.
Nobody knows what nature dreams
Is there anybody still awake?
Keep your head
On the lap of darkness
Try to hear the
Magical sound of night
If you are not hypnotised,
You can hear the
Story of the days foregone.

Existance

The coming days are not for us,
The helpless heart can feel the
Whispering.
All the things we use
And even our body,
Is ready to be sold
To the time upcoming.
Our thoughts are hanged
And displayed as ready
Feelings are confined
Still, our true dreams remain,
To steer our future toward a
Land of peace.

Distance

Though you live in the other hemisphere
The same sun rises and sets.
Love is witnessed
By the sunny day and moonlit night
The backyard is full of dream
Colours of flowers decorate the front
And your home is adorned with things
Of daily use and some show pieces.
When it is winter, you bring out the car
Cutting the layer of ice.
From winter to summer
Car goes a long way
Birthday comes again
Happy and refreshed,
Your mind enjoys with friends
Social media covers the distance.

Rejected Request

Some changes in your mind happened
While I set simply idle.
You came through social media
Eager to get a response.
You called me up, you sent a letter,
And came again and again
Opening your mind
Eager to make me a friend.
But all your requests were rejected
Never calculated it as loss or love.
Simply rejected as my heart
Do not like to respond.
My helpless-self tried to say something
To gear up positivity and possibility,
But dejected from the track
Again and again, you poked me up.
Friendship lost.
But out of all the requests and rejections
Both of us gained a lovely relationship.

Refugee

In the light of Arundhuti,
Standing by the side of the Milky Way,
I tried to search you out.
Rohini knows, that day changes
But love, never.

O my dear, come again,
As the moon rises
to beautify the night sky.
The first bud of the garden
Of my helpless heart till today
Bright enough to shine.
All the creepers in the forest
Drawing a continuous line of love.
But happiness was lost
In the crowd of days forgone
And the mind is homeless in the sky.

Depreciation

Land, Labour, Capital,
And Love combined
Created the Tajmahal – A long-run industry.

Whole life we spend searching for factors
And thousands of combinations are
Used to produce the shape of Iso-quant
Just like a seven-coloured rainbow.

Human wants never stop.
In the indifference map
The ever-increasing addiction
Governs the inevitable struggle
Of the daily accounts.

The carpet of Kashmir covers the construction
With steel, bricks, wood, and stone.
In the differential of time
All travels in the search of
an invisible equilibrium.

Life on 31st

The last day of the year jumping here in its style
The tiny city of India: Kailashahar
Booms with the style of joy,
In the heart of the town, Netaji Corner
decorated with tricolour of the nation's flag.
The Statue of Freedom fighter directs
The way to live the life.

As time demands it,
Now all are free, free to enjoy the nation's freedom
The rush of the marketplace
Showing coat, jacket, jeans, and phiran,
Announcing freedom with foods of different kinds.
The colour of street lights is blue and Vibrant white
mesmerising people on the central road
The tiny city ended the year in its style
All are returning from the outskirts of the city
After a day-long get-together.

The boy settled on the roadside
Came from the Uttar Pradesh to sell
Fried peanuts collected from Rajasthan.
He looks towards the van with rocking music
Coming back from the picnic spot

The boy might remember his home far from the place of
business
It's the last day to step forward and welcome a new year

But still now moonless night showing the Sirius bright
On the eastern horizon.
And the Orion up above that star telling
The story of the long past.
Let us touch the sky-hight of life
Overcoming all the hurdles.
And glide ever on the lap of Mother Nature.